Note to parents, carers and teachers

Read it yourself is a series of modern stories, favourite characters, traditional tales and first reference books, written in a simple way for children who are learning to read. The books can be read independently or as part of a guided reading session.

Each book is carefully structured to include many high-frequency words vital for first reading. The sentences on each page are supported closely by pictures to help with understanding, and to offer lively details to talk about.

The books are graded into four levels that progressively introduce wider vocabulary and longer text as a reader's ability and confidence grows.

Ideas for use

- Although your child will now be progressing towards silent, independent reading, let her know that your help and encouragement is always available.

- Developing readers can be concentrating so hard on the words that they sometimes don't fully grasp the meaning of what they're reading. Answering the quiz questions at the end of the book will help with understanding.

For more information and advice on Read it yourself and book banding, visit **www.ladybird.com/readityourself**

Book Band 9

Level 4 is ideal for children who are ready to read longer stories with a wider vocabulary and are eager to start reading independently.

Special features:

Detailed illustrations capture the imagination

Full exploration of subject

Richer, more varied vocabulary

A long time ago

People learnt to build super structures a long time ago.

Stonehenge, in England, was built about 4,500 years ago.

The Great Pyramid, in Egypt, was built about 4,500 years ago.

People built most of the Great Wall of China 2,000 years ago.

10

11

Longer sentences

Captions offer further explanation

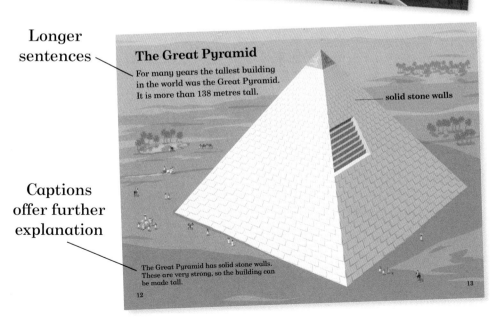

The Great Pyramid

For many years the tallest building in the world was the Great Pyramid. It is more than 138 metres tall.

solid stone walls

The Great Pyramid has solid stone walls. These are very strong, so the building can be made tall.

12

13

Educational Consultant: Geraldine Taylor
Book Banding Consultant: Kate Ruttle
Subject Consultant: Ian Graham

LADYBIRD BOOKS

UK | USA | Canada | Ireland | Australia
India | New Zealand | South Africa

Ladybird Books is part of the Penguin Random House group of companies
whose addresses can be found at global.penguinrandomhouse.com.

www.penguin.co.uk   www.puffin.co.uk   www.ladybird.co.uk

Penguin
Random House
UK

First published 2017
This edition 2019
002

Copyright © Ladybird Books Ltd, 2017

Printed in China

A CIP catalogue record for this book is available from the British Library

ISBN: 978-0-241-40540-6

All correspondence to:
Ladybird Books
Penguin Random House Children's
One Embassy Gardens, 8 Viaduct Gardens, London SW11 7BW

Super Structures

Written by Chris Baker
Illustrated by Stephen Millership

Contents

Super structures

The world has so many super structures. People like to build structures that are big and beautiful.

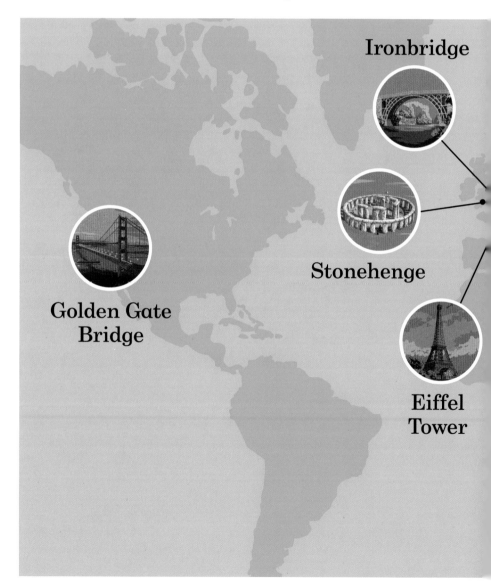

Ironbridge

Stonehenge

Golden Gate Bridge

Eiffel Tower

We will look at these super structures
from around the world.

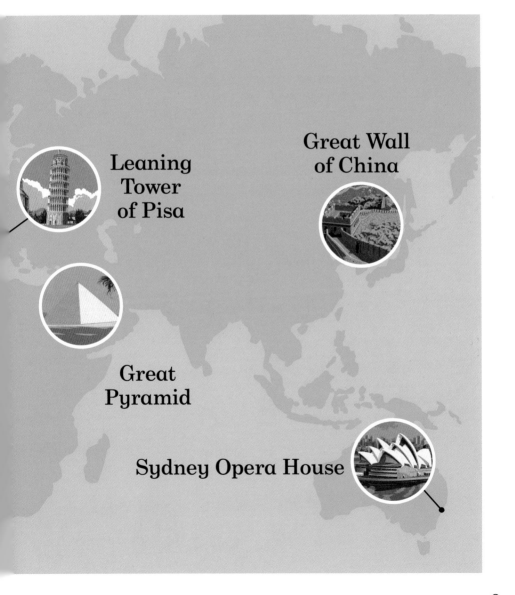

Leaning
Tower
of Pisa

Great Wall
of China

Great
Pyramid

Sydney Opera House

A long time ago

People learnt to build super structures a long time ago.

Stonehenge, in England, was built about 4,500 years ago.

The Great Pyramid, in Egypt, was built about 4,500 years ago.

People built most of the Great Wall
of China 2,000 years ago.

The Great Pyramid

For many years the tallest building in the world was the Great Pyramid. It is more than 138 metres tall.

The Great Pyramid has solid stone walls. These are very strong, so the building can be made tall.

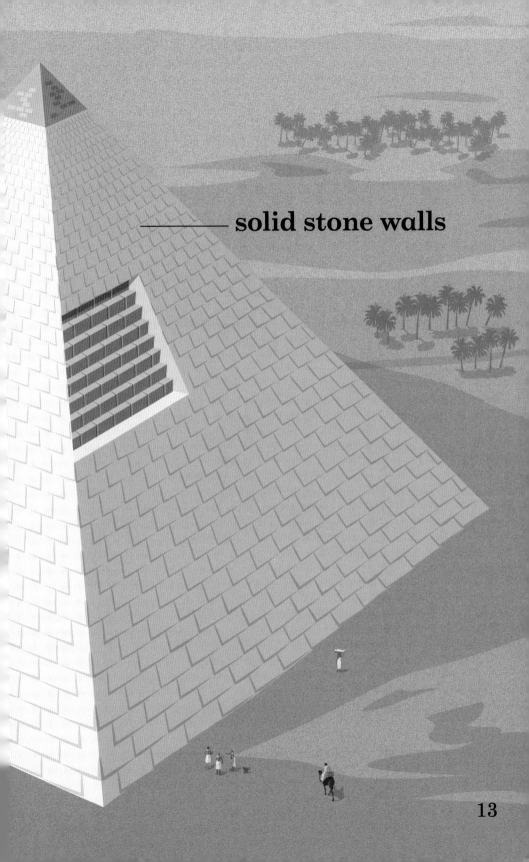

—————— solid stone walls

13

Leaning Tower of Pisa

Tall stone structures are hard to make. They need very solid walls to be strong enough. But solid stone walls can be too heavy.

The Leaning Tower of Pisa, in Italy, is 56 metres tall. It was finished in 1372, but it was too heavy and it began to lean!

15

A new way to make tall structures

One day, William Jenney saw heavy things put down on a little metal cage. It was strong enough to take lots of weight. Now William saw how to make very tall buildings!

William Jenney had an idea.

William Jenney used his idea to build the world's first skyscraper, in the USA, in 1884.

Skyscrapers

Using William Jenney's metal cage idea, people began to build taller and taller skyscrapers.

Skyscrapers are held up by a metal cage inside the structure.

Skyscrapers don't need heavy stone walls. The metal cage inside holds them up, so they can be very tall.

Taller and taller skyscrapers

Using the metal cage idea, people have built taller and taller skyscrapers. No skyscraper has been the tallest for long, because it is not long before people build a taller one!

Tall, taller, tallest – here are some famous skyscrapers.

Built in 1884   **Built in 1902**   **Built in 193**

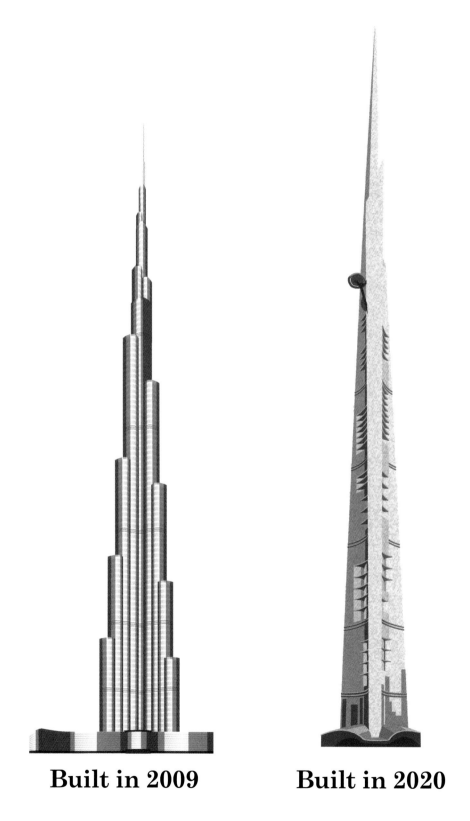

Built in 2009   **Built in 2020**

21

Metal cage structures

Super structures like the Eiffel Tower, in France, are not skyscrapers, but they do use strong metal cages to hold them up and to make them look beautiful.

Eiffel Tower

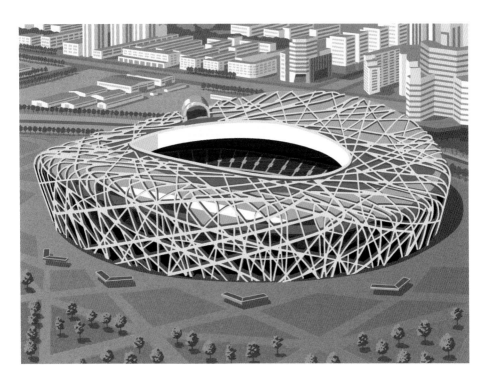

Each of these structures has a metal cage.

Strong bridges

To be strong enough to go across a big gap and not bend, a bridge needs supports.

This bridge can cross a little gap.

But this gap is too big.

This bridge has a support under it.

This bridge has supports to pull it up.

Supports under the bridge

This bridge, in France, was built more than 2,000 years ago to take water across a gap. It is 275 metres long. The bridge is held up by stone supports under it.

Stone supports under the
bridge take the weight.

stone
supports

Rope bridges

This bridge, in Peru, is a suspension bridge. It has no supports under it. Ropes take the weight of the bridge and pull it up.

A bridge has been here for 500 years, but a new rope bridge is made each year. It takes three days to build.

ropes ————

Metal bridges

People learnt how to make
very strong bridges out of metal
and concrete.

Ironbridge, England

Clifton Suspension Bridge, England

Now, bridges can be very long and last for years.

Golden Gate Bridge, USA

Look at the kinds of supports these famous bridges have.

The longest bridge

The Danyang–Kunshan Grand Bridge, in China, is the longest bridge in the world. It has supports under it, and some of it is a suspension bridge.

The Danyang–Kunshan Grand Bridge
is 164 kilometres long!

Bridges that move

Some bridges, like Tower Bridge, in England, can move out of the way so that big things can go under them. The bridge then moves back so people can cross it.

Tower Bridge can move so
that things can go under it.

Super statues

Statues are structures that are made to look like people or other things. Some statues look like famous people. Other statues can be used to show an idea.

Some of the tallest statues around the
world show famous people or ideas.

Concrete structures

Concrete is very strong. It is good at supporting the weight of a structure when the weight is trying to push it down. People have used concrete for a long time.

The big roof on this structure, in Italy, from 2,000 years ago is made of just concrete.

Concrete and metal

Concrete is a very good support against a weight. Metal is strong when a weight is trying to bend it.

We can use concrete and metal together to make big, strong structures, like this dam.

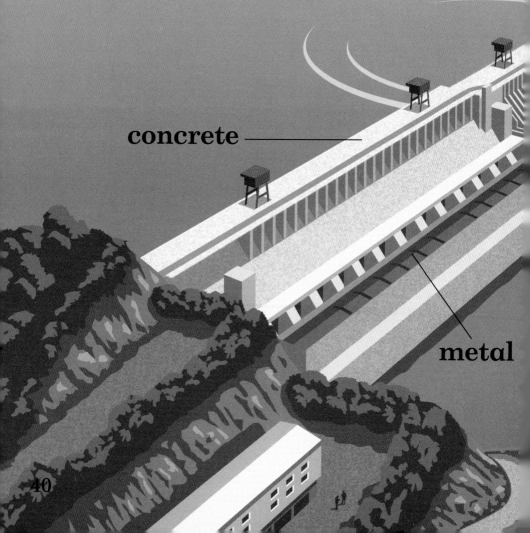

concrete ————

metal

This dam is made of concrete and metal to hold back lots of water.

Sydney Opera House

The Sydney Opera House, in Australia, has a beautiful concrete roof. It was very hard to make this kind of roof out of concrete. It took years to see how to do it.

concrete roof

The Sydney Opera House is one of the world's most beautiful buildings.

43

Picture glossary

 dam

 Eiffel Tower

 Golden Gate Bridge

 Great Pyramid

 Great Wall of China

 Ironbridge

 skyscraper

 statue

 Stonehenge

 supports

 Sydney Opera House

 Tower Bridge

Index

Super Structures quiz

What have you learnt about super structures? Answer these questions and find out!

- What makes the Great Pyramid strong enough to be tall?

- Who invented a way to build skyscrapers?

- What is special about Tower Bridge?

- Where is the longest bridge in the world?

- What is the roof of the Sydney Opera House made of?

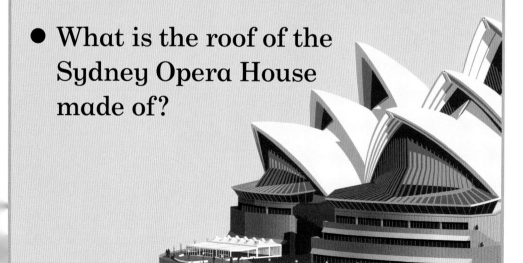

www.ladybird.com